AR
DEVIZES
IN OLD PHOTOGRAPHS

AROUND
DEVIZES
IN OLD PHOTOGRAPHS

COLLECTED BY
DAVID BUXTON

ALAN SUTTON

Alan Sutton Publishing Limited
Phoenix Mill · Far Thrupp · Stroud · Gloucestershire

First published 1990

British Library Cataloguing in Publication Data

Buxton, David *1944–*
Around Devizes in old photographs.
1. Wiltshire, history
I. Title
942.31

ISBN 0-86299-620-1

Typeset in 9/10 Korinna.
Typesetting and origination by
Alan Sutton Publishing Limited.
Printed in Great Britain by
Dotesios Printers Limited.

CONTENTS

ADVERTISEMENTS LIKE THIS ONE often appeared on the reverse of cabinet portrait prints. William Honey succeeded Samuel Marshman, in 1873, at this address and worked there for about twenty years.

INTRODUCTION

Devizes has been an important market town and social centre for a large number of north Wiltshire villages and farms for centuries. This collection of old photographs shows the town engaged in commercial and leisure activities of all kinds during a period of a few decades spanning the turn of the century. It also shows something of the life that went on in some of these villages at that time. Many of these activities are inevitably linked. Although most villages at the end of the nineteenth century were still largely self-supporting they were never totally independent of their nearest market town. Thus, although each village had a baker, a saddler, a blacksmith and so on, there was also the need to attend the local markets to sell produce and buy raw materials for the home and farm. There were also the social attractions of a visit to the town. These pictures include many examples of the market days that were so much more important for everyone then than they are now. The villages have lost their local trades and shops and are, more and more, pretty places to live in and commute to work from. Those old, close-knit village communities where generations of one family lived and worked and everyone knew each other are gone, but existed recently enough to be remembered by many of the older residents. A glimpse of those days can still be gathered in some of these pictures of village life. Some of the pictures may endorse a modern romantic view of life in the old countryside but we should not forget that the truer nature of life in those times was, for most people, very hard indeed. There was also some time for fun. Just see all the pictures of town and village carnivals, fairs and charabanc trips! In fact one could be forgiven for imagining that a lot of time was spent wearing fancy dress and putting up flags until one remembers that the camera was (and still is) brought out much more often for the high days and holidays than for the everyday things in life.

By the turn of the century photography was already over fifty years old and although not as universally popular an amateur activity as it is today was nonetheless a fairly common hobby. It is perhaps surprising then that more amateur photographs from that time do not turn up. Most of the pictures that have survived tend to be commercially produced postcards and prints from professional studios. These are a valuable source but are usually rather formal settings of street scenes and posed studio portraits and much less often informal views of everyday life. It is refreshing then to come across the work of an early amateur as happened when this collection was being assembled. Mr A.J. Hillier was the village blacksmith, first at Horton and later at Bishop's Cannings, and a keen amateur photographer. A few of his photographs taken in about 1900 have survived and are included in this book. There is a picture of his young daughters playing outside the new family house in Bishop's Cannings, a view from the tower of the church and one of the interior, and a rare view of sheep on the downs to the north of the village. A professional studio opened in Devizes as early as 1858 (quite early for a town of its size) and Mr Samuel Marshman appears soon to have prospered judging by the frequency and the confidence of his advertising in the local press and directories. Despite the cumbersome nature of early equipment many photographers of his period must have taken to the road with enthusiasm since series of early postcards exist for even the smallest of villages. It seems likely that early photographers also took advantage of holidays by setting up outdoor studios to record people at their recreation. Judging by the number of pictures one sees of a group posed before Stonehenge (see the one in this book of the Devizes Cycling Club on a day out) this was a good spot to stand with a tripod on a bank holiday!

Salisbury was a convenient stopping place for charabancs heading south to the coast to pause and give their passengers a break. Salisbury photographers must have competed to take their pictures. I have lost count of the number of pictures I have been shown of a Sunday school, village, brewery or choir outing from the Devizes area which was taken not in Devizes, not in the village, not even at the seaside, but in Salisbury!

Most of us enjoy looking at old photographs especially when they depict places and people that we know. The fascination being that it is just a little like it would be if we could travel back in time. In a fraction of a second the camera records a whole scene in all its finest detail and years later we can study the costumes, the hairstyles, the vehicles and even such ephemeral details as the way people posed for a picture or a child played with a hoop. So the old photograph is also potentially an important source for the local and social historian.

An added pleasure I have enjoyed while collecting these photographs has been listening to the stories and memories that usually accompany the unearthing of long-forgotten family photographs. I have noted some of these anecdotes, when appropriate, alongside the photographs. Such memories of days gone by one feels are as important to preserve as the old photographs themselves, but they are much less likely to survive. I have found it useful to take a tape recorder with me on some of my visits and have thus begun another collection of material that adds to the interest and the historical value of the photographs.

SECTION ONE

Town and Market

THE HIGH STREET, Devizes in about 1907, photographed by Whitfield Cosser who had a studio and shop at No. 3. His sign is just visible on the right behind that of T.C. O'Reilly, china and glass merchant. Cosser's premises had already been used for this purpose for about fifty years by a succession of photographers back to Samuel Marshman who opened the first photographic establishment in Devizes there in 1858.

The Market Cross, Devizes.

On Thursday, the 25th January, 1753, Ruth Pierce, of Potterne, in this County, agreed with three other women to buy a sack of wheat in the Market, each paying her due proportion towards the same. One of these women, in collecting the several quotas of money discovered a deficiency, and demanded of Ruth Pierce the sum which was wanting to make good the amount. Ruth Pierce protested that she had paid her share, and said, " She wished she might drop down dead if she had not." She rashly repeated this awful wish, when to the consternation and terror of the surrounding multitude, she instantly fell down and expired, having the money concealed in her hand.

DEVIZES' MOST DISTINCTIVE MONUMENT, the Market Cross, was built in 1814, the gift of Lord Sidmouth, Member of Parliament for Devizes from 1784 to 1805 and Prime Minister from 1801 to 1804. The Shambles indoor market, seen here behind the cross, was rebuilt in 1791 following another donation by him. The inscription borne within one of the arches of the cross and repeated above relates the awful story of Ruth Pierce. A coroner's report of 1753 confirms most of the story but for the final detail. The corporation of 1814 who put up the plaque added in an effort to enhance its moral tone, 'having the money concealed in her hand'.

The Bear Hotel and Corn Exchange.
Devizes.

DEVIZES' FAMOUS OLD COACHING INN, THE BEAR HOTEL, in the Market Place. The Bear dates back to at least 1600 and has been a popular inn for centuries especially during the days of coach and horse. One of its most renowned landlords was Thomas Lawrence who erected signs across Salisbury Plain to guide travellers to the inn. Thomas Lawrence, his son, later a court painter, was a child prodigy and earned a reputation for himself and his father's inn with his precocious drawings of the guests.

THE COACH ENTRANCE at the rear of The Bear Hotel. The use of this entrance continues to the present day although it would have been used less as a main entrance after 1857 when the Corn Exchange was built close alongside it. The hotel's assembly rooms and ballroom were demolished to make room for it and then reconstructed to the rear of the hotel, just outside this picture to the right.

A POSTCARD PICTURE of a water-colour painting of the Market Place that now hangs in the Town Hall. The painting of about 1800 shows the original Market Cross and sign for The Bear Hotel.

NEW PARK ROAD at around the turn of the century. St Mary's church is in the background and the cottage hospital is on the right. The original hospital was built in 1872 and was enlarged several times including additions for each of Queen Victoria's Jubilees in 1877 and 1897.

THESE PHOTOGRAPHS OF SHEEP STREET were taken in the 1950s shortly before the demolition of the whole street. Many of the houses were in a poor state of repair by this time, but the complex of courts and streets that were Old Sheep Street had, until only shortly before, housed a large community of people, which was, by all accounts a colourful one as well. Devizes Library has now replaced the terrace above but some continuity exists between the second picture and the present day. The old hairdresser's shop belonged to Mr Underwood and following demolition was replaced with a new shop that continued to be run by his family.

A BUSY MARKET PLACE in the 1890s.

CHAPEL CORNER is a very old name for the junction of Maryport and Monday Market Streets. In the fourteenth century a chapel for the Priory of the Knights Hospitallers existed here which survived until at least the seventeenth century. Sidmouth Street was Chapel Corner Street until the late eighteenth century and appears as such on Dore's map of Devizes of 1759. The street was also called Leg of Mutton Street for a while. This photograph was taken in the early 1960s.

SIDMOUTH STREET in about 1900. Handel House, the music shop, is just visible on the right and there are still gardens in Albion Place beyond it. The street has been so-called since 1826 when the corporation chose to honour its popular MP Lord Sidmouth.

THE FORMER TOLL-HOUSE, now called Shane's Castle, at the junction of the Chippenham and Bath Roads out of Devizes seen here in about 1905.

THE END OF SIDMOUTH STREET showing the house, shop and abattoir of Walter Rose and Sons butchers in about 1922.

A SUNNY MORNING ON THE GREEN photographed by John Chivers in about 1905.

LONG STREET, DEVIZES, in about 1900.

DEVIZES MARKET PLACE about 1900.

A QUIET DAY IN THE MARKET PLACE in the mid-1930s.

SOUTHBROOM ROAD at the corner of Pans Lane in about 1920.

HILLWORTH HOUSE AND HILLWORTH ROAD in the early years of the century. This road originally followed the edge of an outer defensive ditch of the castle and was known as Gallows Ditch because it reputedly led to the site of the town gallows at the point where Estcourt Hill now meets Hillworth Road.

A PHOTOGRAPH OF SIDMOUTH STREET in about 1900, showing Holland's tobacconist's shop (later E.F. Duck) at the end, on the left, and behind it the old Town School. The last shop on the right was T.H. White's (agricultural engineers) first premises and in the foreground is the old Unicorn Hotel. Although the Unicorn is no longer a hotel the old bracket that held the inn sign still remains on the building today.

THE CRAMMER POND ON THE GREEN in the early years of the century. The origin of the pond and its name are uncertain. The pond was probably man-made in early castle times as a fish stock pond. It has no natural stream and relies on rain to fill it. It is possible that the name comes from an Anglo-Saxon word for fairground stalls and booths, *Krames*. The Green has for centuries been a place where seasonal fairs are held. The tall building in the picture is Wild's Brewery, which later became the fire station and finally the offices of W.E. Chivers, the builders. It was demolished in 1990.

DEVIZES WAS ONE OF THE FOUR HOLDERS OF THE COUNTY QUARTER SESSIONS for the Assizes from the fourteenth century. This photograph shows a procession taking the judge through the Market Place to the Assize Courts in Northgate Street in the early years of this century. Handel House in Sidmouth Street was the official residence of judges during the Assizes in the first half of the nineteenth century.

NORTHGATE STREET, DEVIZES, in about 1900. The Ionic columns of T.H. Wyatt's Assize Courts (built in 1835) are visible on the right.

THE MARKET PLACE in about 1950. The central area is by this time well established as a car park and concrete lamp-posts have arrived.

MARKET DAY IN DEVIZES in the early 1950s.

THE BATH ROAD, DEVIZES, in about 1910.

A LEAFY DUNKIRK HILL about 1900 with Shane's Castle just visible at the top.

A BUSY THURSDAY MARKET in Devizes in about 1912. Motor vehicles have by this time started to appear as more common modes of transport, even a huge Dennis motor bus, but horse-drawn traffic would still have been the norm for most people.

THIS VIEW OF THE MARKET PLACE was taken in the 1940s, possibly just after the war. Although the presence of poultry in cages suggest a market day the absence of other stalls, except for a man selling something from a suitcase to passing servicemen, makes this a bit doubtful.

CHARLIE STONE FROM URCHFONT AND MR FRY FROM BREMHILL chat at Devizes cattle market in the early 1940s.

SIDMOUTH STREET from the junction with Estcourt Street photographed in about 1910. The shop on the facing corner had only recently been completed by the firm of W.E. Chivers when this was taken. It was demolished in 1989 to widen the road.

LONG STREET in about 1905.

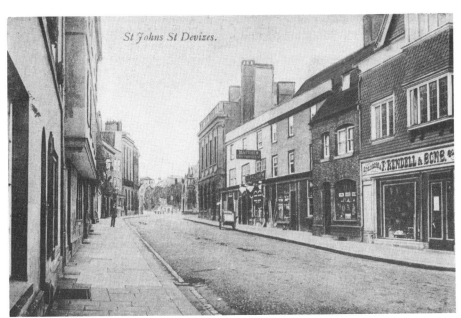

ST JOHN'S STREET, Devizes, in about 1910.

SECTION TWO

Churches
and Big Houses

SPYE PARK HOUSE, NEAR BROMHAM, about 1900. The house was built in the 1860s for the Spicer family who remained the owners until the house was demolished in 1987.

ST MARY'S CHURCH, BISHOP'S CANNINGS, photographed in about 1900 by the village blacksmith, Mr A.J. Hillier. The church is Early English in style and had a spire added in the fifteenth century. There is also a curious little steeple next to the spire that predates the latter and is in fact a stair turret for access to the tower. Traditionally this little steeple is said to have been the subject for teasing of the inhabitants by residents of Devizes and the surrounding area who suggested that the steeple, like the people of the village, was somehow ridiculous and immature. Driven by exasperation some inhabitants are reputed to have carried a load of manure up the tower to plant around the steeple which, when it became known, only served to increase the ridicule. For many years it was the custom for Cannings farmers to be greeted at Devizes Market with, 'Hast dunged thy little steeple yet?'

THE INTERIOR OF BISHOP'S CANNINGS CHURCH in about 1900. Just visible are the fourteenth-century font and the carved pew ends, each one different. The lighting is by oil lamps.

ALMOST NOTHING REMAINS OF THE ORIGINAL DEVIZES CASTLE built in the early part of the twelfth century by Bishop Roger, right-hand man to Henry I. Only the moat and the mound remain on which now stands this fanciful Victorian creation. Valentine Leach, a Devizes draper, started the building in the 1840s and it was enlarged over the next forty years by his son. This photograph dates from about 1900.

*Blount's Court
Potterne*

BLOUNT'S COURT, a large Victorian Gothic mansion was built in 1870 by William Stancomb. It is seen here in the early years of the century and is today divided into flats. The Stancomb family revived an old name for the house and estate. In the thirteenth century Geoffrey Le Blunt held lands in Potterne. In 1530 the manor of Potterne was referred to as Bluntty's Court and by 1570 as Blount's Court.

BROMHAM CHURCH OF ST NICHOLAS seen here in about 1900. The trees in the churchyard are now so large as to almost obscure the church from view. The church has a south chapel of 1492 which is highly decorated and reminiscent of the contemporary Beauchamp Chapel at St John's church in Devizes, and a stained-glass window by William Morris.

THE GRANGE, WORTON, a large timber-framed house originally built in the early seventeenth century but much restored, probably at the end of the last century.

THE MAGNIFICENT TIMBER-FRAMED HOUSE KNOWN AS TALBOYS in Keevil, seen here in a late-Victorian photograph. Although the main part of the house was built in the late fifteenth century the left-hand wing is a Victorian addition.

THE WESLEYAN CHAPEL IN LONG STREET photographed here soon after it was built in 1898.

Monument in St. John's
Churchyard, Devizes.

Inscriptions on the Monument.

1st. In memory of the sudden
and awful end of Robert Merritt
and Susannah, his wife, Eliz.
Tilley, her sister Martha Carter
and Josiah Derham, who were
all drowned in the flower of their
youth in a Pond near this Town,
called Drews, on Sunday Evening,
30th June, 1751, and are together
underneath entombed.

2nd. This Monument as a
solemn Monitor to young people
to remember their Creator in the
days of their youth was erected
by subscription.

3rd. Remember the Sabbath
Day to keep it Holy.

THIS MONUMENT STILL STANDS in St John's churchyard although the inscription on it is now difficult to read. Its legend tells of the 'sudden and awful end' of five young Devizes people in 1751. This picture and details of the inscription are from a Victorian postcard.

ST JOHN'S CHURCH, built in the mid-twelfth century as the garrison church for the castle, retains much of its original Norman architecture. This picture from 1861 shows the west front before restoration.

THE WEST FRONT OF ST JOHN'S CHURCH following complete restoration and rebuilding in 1861.

NEW PARK STREET in about 1907. Brownston House, on the right, was built in 1720 and is considered by many to be one of Devizes' finest houses.

BROWNSTON HOUSE seen from the back in about 1900.

ST MARY'S CHURCH was originally built to serve the new town that grew outside the Norman castle's defences in the mid-twelfth century. It is possible that the church on this site predates St John's, the castle church, but retains less of its Norman architecture than the latter. Much of the exterior dates from the fifteenth century although there is a fine Norman chancel inside.

THE SOUTH PORCH OF ST MARY'S CHURCH, Devizes, probably photographed at the same time as those showing the restoration of St John's were taken.

POTTERNE HIGH STREET looking north with fourteenth-century Porch House in the middle and the beautiful timber-framed Porch Cottages in the foreground.

THE DINING HALL OF PORCH HOUSE.

THE GARDENS TO THE REAR OF PORCH HOUSE as they were in about 1910. Excavations here suggest that there was possibly a very early (tenth-century) timber-framed church on this site, which may also have been the original home of the Saxon stone font now in St Mary's church.

ST MATTHEW'S CHURCH, ROWDE in the early years of the century. The church was largely rebuilt in 1833 and now only the high tower remains of the previous fifteenth-century building.

BATTLE HOUSE, BROMHAM in about 1911. Formerly the Dower House of the ancient Manor of Bromham. Battle is a name that dates back to the eleventh century when William II gave Bromham to Battle Abbey to which it belonged until 1538. The house was, for a time, the home of the pre-war *Punch* cartoonist Leonard Ravenhill (see p. 115).

SEEND CHURCH bears evidence of the village's early association with the cloth trade. John Stokes a wealthy fifteenth-century clothier built the north aisle and in the west window moulding clothier's shears and scissors are carved. There is a brass monument to him and his wife. This photograph is from a postcard of about 1900.

Potterne Church.

THE CHURCH OF ST MARY, POTTERNE, is a good example of the Early English style. It has been barely altered or added to since the thirteenth century.

SLOPERTON COTTAGE, BROMHAM, photographed here in about 1900, was home of the Irish poet Thomas Moore who died and was buried in Bromham churchyard in 1852.

POULSHOT CHURCH.

ST PETER'S CHURCH, POULSHOT, about 1900 and before the disastrous fire of 1916. The church is largely thirteenth-century with a mid-nineteenth century tower. The church probably originally served Poulshot and Worton which would explain its remoteness from the centre of both villages. The walk of nearly a mile from Poulshot must have tested the resolve of villagers over the years and by the end of the last century congregations were so small that an alternative place of worship was built on the green. The small, simple chapel of ease (opposite) was initially used for occasional services but its popularity was such that it was soon used more than the church. On 2 February 1916 the church was to have been used for a wedding and because there had not been a service there for several months the caretaker went to the church early in the morning to light the stove and tidy up. At midday a passing farmer noticed smoke pouring from the roof and sounded the alarm. A badly corroded chimney pipe was blamed for the fire which had started between the ceiling and the roof and was so well established by the time the Devizes fire brigade arrived that little could be done. The roof of the nave, its windows and most of the contents were lost. The wedding pair were married at the chapel of ease.

ST PETER'S CHURCH, POULSHOT, after the fire in 1916. Only a few months before the fire a church committee had decided not to renew the church insurance because of the high cost of the premium. It was not until 1926 that sufficient funds had been raised to complete the extensive repairs and bring the church back into use. This was perhaps a remarkable achievement when one considers how little the church was used prior to the fire.

THE CHAPEL OF EASE built on Poulshot Green in 1897 as an alternative place of worship to the remote village church. After the church fire it was the sole place for Anglican worship for ten years but continued in occasional use right up to the 1960s and then served as the village hall.

ROUNDWAY HOUSE, seen here from the north side, was the home of the Colston family from 1840 until 1948. C.G.H.A. Colston became Lord Roundway in 1916. The house and estate lie close to Roundway village, about one mile north of Devizes, and were formerly owned by the Devizes MP Thomas Southeron Estcourt. Most of the house was demolished in the early 1950s.

THE KENNELS ON ROUNDWAY ESTATE which housed Lord Roundway's hounds. The Roundway Foot Harriers, dressed in green jackets with red collars, hunted hares on foot.

SECTION THREE

Shops and Businesses

COOK'S THE BUTCHERS in the High Street, in about 1928. This shop was lost when the Gateway supermarket was built, but the firm continued in new premises a little higher up the street.

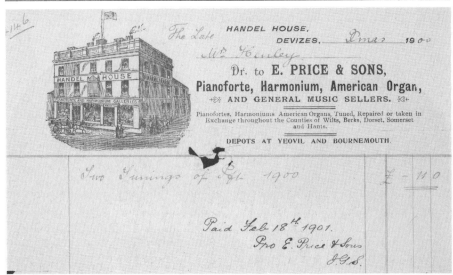

HANDEL HOUSE,
DEVIZES,

Dr. to E. PRICE & SONS,
Pianoforte, Harmonium, American Organ,
AND GENERAL MUSIC SELLERS.

Pianofortes, Harmoniums American Organs, Tuned, Repaired or taken in
Exchange throughout the Counties of Wilts, Berks, Dorset, Somerset
and Hants.

DEPOTS AT YEOVIL AND BOURNEMOUTH.

HANDEL HOUSE AT THE CORNER OF SIDMOUTH STREET AND SHEEP STREET was for many years the head office and main shop of one of the largest music businesses in the south and west. E. Price and Sons converted the old judges' lodgings into a showroom and workshops in 1872 and the building continued in this use for nearly a hundred years. The firm had branches in many towns in Wiltshire and adjacent counties and it appears that they were all named Handel House. This old letter-head shows the cost of two piano tunings in 1900. The building is now a bookshop and fine art gallery, and the older building behind it, in Price's day the music workshop, is now a restaurant.

A DISPLAY IN ONE OF THE GRAND WIN-DOWS OF HANDEL HOUSE in the 1930s. The display of the latest Columbia, 78 rpm record releases is enhanced by a stuffed lion holding a record in its mouth under the slogan, 'Music soothes the savage beast'.

A GROUP OF APPRENTICES outside the Sheep Street workshop of Handel House in about 1928. Second from left is Geoffrey Oliver who was later to manage the business and to his left is Bill Smith who, at the time of writing, is still involved in the music business in Devizes.

INSIDE THE MUSIC SHOP in about 1936. Peggy Oliver and Hilda Bond pose for a photograph behind the record counter.

THE HANDEL HOUSE MUSIC BUSINESS not only sold, tuned and repaired musical instruments but also made them. William Robinson, from Avebury, was a violin maker and is seen here in 1943 at the workshops in Sheep Street, watched by a young Michael Oliver, son of the proprietor. Michael was later to play the violin that hangs behind him in this picture.

THE THREE CROWNS BREWERY and pub in Maryport Street decorated for the coronation of George V in 1911. The brewery, owned by the Phipps family since the 1860s, was reported to have 'the prettiest and most effective decorations in the West of England'. Mrs Phipps made all the 6,000 paper flowers used herself and decorated the four first-floor windows as Spring, Summer, Autumn and Winter.

JOHN CHIVERS, A DEVIZES PHOTOGRAPHER ('photographic artist'), who had a studio in Sidmouth Street, from 1898 until about 1925. This cabinet print, taken in his own studio, is probably from about 1900. Many of his portraits and town photographs are well-known.

THIS VIEW OF THE MARKET PLACE is taken from an old promotional postcard for Simpsons the grocers shop at No. 42 next to the Shambles. Simpsons was a general grocer still remembered by some people in Devizes. This card was delivered to a Long Street address, probably with a grocery order since it was not stamped, and bears on the reverse a number of 'Useful Summer Lines'. One could have chosen from Cambridge Lemonade 5½d., Seedhouse's Gingerette 5d., Feltoe's Lime Juice 1s. 1d., Carter's Lemon Syrup 1s. 2d., or Birk's Junket Powder 3d. and 6d.

STRATTON, SONS AND MEAD'S WAREHOUSE in Monday Market Street in about 1910. This large wholesale grocery firm was established in Devizes in 1902 and supplied retail shops all over Wiltshire and adjacent counties. There was also a retail shop in this building. A large staff was employed as travelling sales representatives, office staff to process the orders and warehousemen to pack and deliver the goods.

THE MANAGER'S OFFICE at Stratton, Sons and Mead.

TWO PHOTOGRAPHS SHOWING STAFF AT STRATTON, SONS AND MEAD'S in the 1920s. These photographs suggest contrasting work styles and privileges for the office staff and warehouse staff at this time. The older men in their heavy coats were probably outdoor workers and were possibly involved with the care of the delivery horses or the deliveries themselves.

THE PELICAN INN IN THE MARKET PLACE in about 1905. We don't grow window boxes like they used to do!

SLADE'S BASKET AND HARDWARE SHOP in the Market Place has closed and gone recently enough for most people in Devizes to remember it well. These photographs were taken shortly before the shop closed in the late 1970s. A basket and brush shop had been here for a long time; see the shop in the view of the Market Place on p. 87 taken in the 1890s.

Display of Jams and push of
Iced Fruit Cake 7ᵈ lb.

All Branches will arrange this display on **Monday, October 3rd.** The display will run for **one week.**

This display is set out in a 7-ft. 6-in. window with a back shelf 9-ins. high.

The centre stack of Jam is raised on a corned beef box.

The central display of cake is raised on pedestals 1, 2 and 3 tins high.

Please see that the cut halves of cake are neatly wrapped in cellophane.

The jars must be highly polished to get the best effect.

37460—100733   **International Tea Co.'s Stores, Ltd.**

THE INTERNATIONAL STORES in the Brittox, like all other branches of the company in the land received weekly instruction sheets like this one. Not only was each shop to promote the same products at the same time but to assemble the window in exactly the same fashion. Display cards and price indicators also arrived in the weekly pack to complete the uniformity. This one went on show on 3 October 1938.

THE INTERNATIONAL STORES at the end of the Brittox, photographed in 1923. The staff, from the left, were: Miss Tadd, Miss Ruddle, Lionel Hailstone, Mr Knight, young Mr Harris and Albert Yates.

THE TIMBER YARD AND SAWMILLS of W.E. Chivers and Sons at Nursteed Road in 1920 with one of the largest gantry cranes in the south of England.

INSIDE ONE OF THE SAWMILL SHEDS at W.E. Chivers and Sons showing the steam-powered saw.

DURING THE FIRST WORLD WAR W.E. Chivers was not only the haulage contractor but also supplied materials for the Army. Here The Green is being used to store large quantities of timber and wooden, prefabricated army huts prior to despatch.

THE BARRACKS POST OFFICE in London Road, Devizes, used to be in a terrace of houses opposite Le Marchant Barracks and was much used by the soldiers. This photograph of about 1910 shows Miss Richardson in the doorway when she was assistant postmistress.

TO SEE THE VILLAGE OF SEEND TODAY it is hard to believe that less than a century ago it was a centre for heavy industry, with mining for iron ore and an ironworks to smelt it. Although the existence of iron ore had been known for a long time (John Aubrey referred to it in the seventeenth century), it was not until the late nineteenth century that commerical attempts were made to exploit it. The arrival of canal and railway made it possible to transport the ore (10,000 tons went to Bristol by canal in 1856), and later to bring fuel for smelting it to Seend. Smelting the ore locally was never a great success. Between 1857 and 1888 no less than five companies in turn were set up and bankrupted by the ironworks. Three blast furnaces and a rail link to Seend station were built and at its peak of activity, when this picture was taken in 1870 the works employed 300 men and produced 300 tons of iron a week. By 1876 the blast furnaces had been abandoned but extraction of ore continued for many years, only finally coming to an end in the 1940s.

SLOPER'S DEPARTMENT STORE in the Brittox in 1929. The shop-fronts, including those on the extreme right, had been extensively altered in this year. The modernization included recessing the ground and first-floor frontage, a feature which has been retained to the present day by Woolworth's and Boots, who now occupy these premises.

SECTION FOUR

Transport

ALFRED HAILSTONE was appointed a sales representative for Wadworth's Brewery in about 1914 and got a car with the job. Although he stands very proudly with his foot on the running-board of a fine French Rollaid-Pilain (1908), he could not drive, so Wadworth's supplied a chauffeur.

THE NEW INN on the Devizes to Melksham road at Seend in about 1905. This pub is now called The Three Magpies.

THE BODMAN FAMILY began a coach and charabanc business in Worton in 1922 and still operate the present business from the same garage in High Street, Worton. The business began in the former blacksmith's premises vacated by Mr Goss when he moved to the Rose and Crown further up the street. Here is Mrs Dunford in about 1928 with an early Bodman bus. Mrs Dunford drove buses and coaches for the firm for fifty years and has many tales to tell of her driving experiences.

PIPE LAYING IN POTTERNE HIGH STREET in about 1905. The contractor was Henry Ash of Devizes and the man with the beard in the foreground is the site foreman, Albert Smith.

WILSON CARLILE founded the Church Army in 1882 as a Church of England mission to the working classes. Travelling waggons like this one arriving in Potterne in about 1900 conducted roadside services anywhere, from remote villages to the big cities.

THIS PHOTOGRAPH AND THE FOLLOWING THREE show the development of Ward's Garage in New Park Street. This one taken in 1907 of The Devizes Garage shows a selection of cars for sale including from left to right, a 1905 Rover Phaeton, 1907 Rover Twenty and 1902 Panhard et Levassor. Mr Ward also had a garage in Northgate Street and a shop in the Brittox at this time. He was a close friend of Billy Morris, later Lord Nuffield, and was appointed as only the third Morris dealer in the country.

WARD'S MOTORS IN NEW PARK STREET in 1933; by this time the business had been acquired by Bill Drinkwater who had joined Mr Ward as an employee in 1903. The cars for sale in the showroom are a Morris Twelve and a Morris Ten.

WARD'S MOTORS IN NEW PARK STREET in 1958. Although the name was retained it had been acquired in 1954 by Bath Garages.

WARD'S MOTORS IN NEW PARK STREET in 1962.

PART OF THE FAMOUS CAEN HILL FLIGHT OF TWENTY-NINE LOCKS on the Kennet and Avon Canal looking up the hill to Devizes. The canal was opened in 1810 and provided a navigable link between the Avon and the Thames from which trade in Devizes benefited considerably. Competition from the railway, which arrived in Devizes in 1862 inevitably led to a decline in its importance but it remained in regular use well into this century. After many years of dereliction the Caen Hill flight of locks was finally restored and reopened for use in 1990.

THE LOCK-KEEPER'S HOUSE on the Caen Hill flight of locks.

ONE OF A LARGE FLEET OF STEAM ENGINES (with a mascot) owned by W.E. Chivers and Sons. The firm was a major national haulage company and during the First World War were main haulage contractors to the Army. They had steam-engine depots in Sheffield, Leeds and London.

ALFRED HAILSTONE in 1916 was a travelling representative for Stratton's the wholesale grocers in Monday Market Street, Devizes. Doing the rounds of the village shops in a pony and a trap sounds, at least in the summer, a pleasant enough occupation. He is seen here with an apprentice on the Andover road near Wedhampton.

DEVIZES STATION opened in 1857 when a branch line connected Devizes to the Wilts. Somerset and Weymouth Railway. It was linked up to the east via Hungerford five years later with an extension to the Berks. and Hants. Railway. The arrival of a rail link to Devizes opened up many new possibilities for trade and a good passenger link to London. The station and branch line were unfortunately closed in 1966. This picture shows an old pannier tank engine (built in Swindon in 1932) arriving at platform one in 1958.

IN THE LATTER PART OF THE LAST CENTURY and early part of this one the station was very busy and employed a large staff. Here are a few of them grouped on the edge of platform one in about 1895.

A SMALL GOODS ENGINE takes on water and then steams past the signal box at Devizes station in the winter of 1962.

A STEAM TRAIN LEAVING DEVIZES, photographed in about 1920 from the Nursteed Road as it passes between Stert and Nursteed.

TWO MILK TANKERS like this one delivered Wiltshire milk to London in 1927. Based in Bulkington they collected milk from farms around Devizes and made the slow journey to London each day at a maximum speed of 12 m.p.h. The tankers were made by a firm called Maudslay and the glass-lined tanks came from Denmark.

SECTION FIVE

Men in Uniform

THE ROYAL WILTSHIRE YEOMANRY, 'the Prince of Wales' own', present the winning team in the Regimental Troop Sword Competition of 1900. Centre of the back row is their instructor Sgt. Major Bagshaw; behind him is The Bear Hotel.

THE DEVIZES POLICE FORCE in the 1870s. The style of hat worn here was replaced by the more familiar helmet in about 1880. The senior officer, who wears a top hat, is saved the problem faced by the other constables of where to put the chin strap when sporting a full beard. A constable on the right is holding what appears to be a white cat; was he showing the force's mascot or perhaps keeping secure a valuable piece of evidence while the photograph was taken?

AN OFFICIAL POLICE VEHICLE of the Devizes police station in about 1890.

THE TROWBRIDGE FIRE BRIGADE seen here in the early 1920s with a new fire engine displayed on the lawns of Seend House, home of the Brigade's chairman, Mr Usher the brewer.

A PEACEFUL VIEW OF THE LONDON ROAD and Le Marchant Barracks taken before the First World War.

A SQUAD OF NEW RECRUITS to the Wiltshire Regiment photographed at the end of their three months' training at Le Marchant Barracks in 1934. The man who was responsible for them during training was Sgt. Thurston who is seated in the middle of the front row.

THE MILITARY HOSPITAL at Le Marchant Barracks in Devizes some time between 1910 and 1915.

THE OPENING CEREMONY of the Wiltshire Regiment's Cottage Homes in Devizes in 1904. This pair of houses, on the London Road at the edge of town, was built with subscriptions from the regiment as a memorial to Prince Christian Victor and officers and men who died in the war in South Africa between 1899 and 1902. The houses were to be used by disabled men of the regiment and still provide a home for one ex-soldier, Mr William Stanley, and his wife. The houses are administered now by Lord Robert's Forces Aid Society.

DURING THE FIRST WORLD WAR groups of Royal Engineers were trained in the use of canal boats in preparation for the invasion of occupied France and Belgium. Here a team acquire canal skills on the Kennet and Avon Canal at Devizes. Two barges are turning round in the stretch between the town lock and Prison Bridge. In the background is the enclosure of the old swimming pool.

NEGOTIATING THE LOCKS on a day that looks as cold and wet as the canal itself.

SOLDIERS WITH CANAL HORSES at Devizes Wharf.

OPENING THE LOCK GATES AT TOWN LOCK by the bridge in Northgate Street under the watchful eyes of the old lock keeper and the commanding officer (who probably posed for St Bruno advertisements in his spare time).

DEVIZES FIRE BRIGADE MOVED TO ESTCOURT STREET to occupy a converted building next to the Bell Inn, formerly Wild's Brewery, in 1924. The building, owned by W.E. Chivers, was leased for £40 per year. The chairman of the brigade at this time was Councillor Frank Chivers, coal merchant, seen here second from the right.

DEVIZES FIRE BRIGADE using foam on a petrol tanker carrying aviation fuel that threatened to catch fire by the Clock Inn at Lydeway near Urchfont in 1939. In fact 'the fire' was apparently an overheated brake drum and this may have been just the opportunity the fire brigade had been waiting for to try out their brand new foam equipment.

SECTION SIX

Children

THE SECOND CLASS of 1912 at Poulshot First School on the village green. Miss Jones was the teacher and among the pinafored girls were two Annies, two Emilys, Floss, Gladys, Dolly, Elsie and Kit. The stiff-collared boys included Alf, Bert, Reg and Jack. Poulshot school was built in 1884 and was in use until 1974. After this date village children attended Rowde School and the former school became the village hall.

SIR JOHN EVERETT MILLAIS' PAINTING of a small boy blowing bubbles was immensely popular with the Victorians and through mass-produced prints was a familiar sight on the walls of many homes. When Pears Soap began to use the picture in their advertisements in 1885, suitably modified to include a bar of their soap, it caused a sensation. This pastiche of the picture made around 1900 was set up and photographed in Devizes by John Chivers in his studio in Sidmouth Street.

MARSH LANE, ROWDE, LOOKING TOWARDS THE HIGH STREET. On the left is the Wesleyan Chapel, built in 1838 and now a private house.

A PAGEANT OR PLAY PUT ON BY CHILDREN OF POTTERNE SCHOOL as part of the village's celebrations at the coronation in 1911.

A WAR EFFORT FUND-RAISING EVENT in Worton during the Second World War with children dressed as nurses and battle victims. The horse was led by Lily Oram, a Land Army girl.

SCHOOLBOYS AT WORTON SCHOOL in 1910 learning some rural skills.

THE HOME OF MR A.J. HILLIER, THE BLACKSMITH in Bishop's Cannings, in about 1905. The forge is just visible on the left and his three daughters are outside, including baby Marjorie in the whicker pram. George Formby was a regular visitor to the forge when he was training to be a jockey at the local stables. He grew too big for riding and left for a career elsewhere for which he was to become rather more famous.

MARKET DAY IN DEVIZES in about 1895.

THE HILLIER GIRLS AT BISHOP'S CANNINGS in about 1906. When they were a little older they would take this pony and trap regularly into Devizes.

URCHFONT SUNDAY SCHOOL CLASS outside the church in 1919. The teacher was Miss Ada Mabel Emma Lyne who taught at the Sunday school for many years. She was of very small stature with very short limbs.

AN OUTING ON THE KENNET AND AVON CANAL to Horton by St John's church Sunday school, Devizes, in 1918.

ROWDE SCHOOL IN MARSH LANE in about 1908. The present school has several modern extensions to this building, which was itself built in 1908 as a substantial extension to an earlier school of 1841.

A SCHOOL FÊTE AT WORTON SCHOOL in the early 1920s produced some patriotic costumes, including several wartime uniforms re-emerging as fancy dress.

A CLASS OF GIRLS AT SOUTHBROOM SCHOOL by the Crammer in Devizes in 1922.

A BOAT TRIP ON THE KENNET AND AVON CANAL was a popular Sunday school outing for local children. This one shows a party about to disembark for a picnic in the field where tables and food have already arrived by road.

CHILDREN OF PARNELLA SCHOOL photographed in 1929. Parnella School was founded in 1870 by Miss Davies and took its name from Parnella House in the Market Place which it occupied for most of its existence, although it started and ended in different houses in Long Street. It closed in 1937. The headmistress in this picture (centre) is Miss Springford who taught music, on her right is Miss Britain who taught the five- to eleven-year-olds and on her left Miss Staines who taught the eleven- to sixteen-year-old girls. Boys left at eleven years. The picture was taken in the garden at Parnella House.

MRS OLIVER'S SHOP, at the top of the Brittox opposite Charles Sloper & Son (reflections of the blinds are visible in the window), sold toys and children's clothes but of more interest to many children in the town she held tea parties in the shop for small numbers of favoured children. She sent invitations to schoolchildren to what she called a 'Live Doll's Tea Party' which would be held in the window of the shop. A small crowd of envious onlookers usually gathered outside hoping for an invitation to the next one. This one took place in 1916.

IN THE EARLY YEARS OF THE LAST WAR thousands of London children were evacuated to the country in an attempt to save them from the bombs. Although the effort must have saved many lives, the separation and culture shock for many of the children (and their parents) must have been great. This group of London evacuees suddenly found themselves billetted with village families in Worton in 1939. They were educated, not in the village school with local children, but in the village hall taught by a series of part-time teachers. They look fairly cheerful here, having lessons on the grass by the church. One of these children returned after the war and still lives in Worton.

THE CHILDREN OF POTTERNE SCHOOL line up for a photograph before setting off for a day at the seaside in about 1950.

'LIBRARY HOUR', Urchfont village school, in the 1920s.

MISS WESTON WITH THE INFANTS' CLASS at Bishop's Cannings School in 1936. Schools at nearby Coate and Horton closed in the 1920s and '30s respectively and children from these villages then attended Bishop's Cannings School.

THE CHILDREN OF POULSHOT CELEBRATE KING GEORGE V'S CORONATION in 1911 with an open-air tea.

THESE TWO PICTURES SHOW BOYS OF THE DEVIZES GRAMMAR SCHOOL performing a gymnastic display in about 1912. This school was founded in 1871 by Revd S.S. Pugh, minister at the New Baptist Chapel, and until 1920 was at Heathcote House on The Green.

SECTION SEVEN

Sport and Leisure

E. AND W. ANSTIE'S FOOTBALL TEAM of the 1900/1 season. Anstie's tobacco factory in the Market Place made snuff, cigarettes and cigars for over two hundred years, finally closing in 1961. Second from left, with an impressive moustache, is the team's president Mr E. C. Anstie and on the right is their vice-president, the more casually dressed Mr G.E. Anstie.

BULKINGTON CHURCH CHOIR OUTING in 1926 was to Weymouth by charabanc. The speed limit on the side of the bus says 12 m.p.h.

VILLAGE CARNIVALS were a highlight of the year and were often recorded in photographs. Urchfont carnivals of the 1920s are depicted in a series of numbered postcards. Here is one, a decorated horse and cart from 1923.

THIS DECORATED FLOAT in the Urchfont carnival of 1923 was Charles Stones' baker's cart. The driver was Jack Harris and the 'baker', George Waite.

SOME OF THE ENTRANTS for the fancy dress competition in Urchfont carnival in 1923.

THE LATE NINETEENTH CENTURY was something of a heyday for cycling and there were many cycling clubs who spent weekends and holidays exploring the countryside. Here is the Devizes Cycling Club on a day's excursion to Stonehenge in 1895.

A RETIRED FILM DIRECTOR, BASIL ROSCOE, moved into Wedhampton Manor in the mid-1930s and soon after set up The Urchfont and Chirton Players. He produced several revues in Urchfont village hall. This scene from 'Spotlight 1936' has two male members of The Players dressed as nannies in a comedy routine.

MEGAN WILLIAMS sings 'Home James' in an Urchfont village hall revue of 1934.

102

THE GRECIAN CHORUS from Basil Roscoe's 'Spotlight 1936' at Urchfont village hall.

AUNT POLLY, with the reins, takes some friends for a ride in Bulkington in 1910.

FAIRGROUND ENTERTAINMENT has been associated with Devizes since Henry Jennings first began to provide 'rides' at agricultural shows in the area at the end of the nineteenth century. The Jennings family still operate their fairs from Devizes. This is the traction engine known as *Royal John*, built by Wallis and Stevens, that was used to power and illuminate the Jennings' galloper roundabout.

WILLIAM TAYLOR, AN EARLY ASSOCIATE OF HENRY JENNINGS, who frequently toured with him, brought this travelling cinematograph show to Devizes. The magnificently painted and gilded façade with its lights and organ attracted a crowd who were then to be enticed inside to watch a short moving picture show. Built into the structure on the right is the large traction engine, *Victoria*, built by Burrells in 1906, which provided the power for the lights, the organ and the show.

PART OF THE ENTERTAINMENT before one of William Taylor's cinematograph shows would include music and dancing. Here Taylor's daughters, Marie and Harriet (centre), and their cousins perform one of their routines that was intended to draw crowds to the show.

BISHOP'S CANNINGS FOOTBALL TEAM of 1897. Village football at this time was very popular and strong sides competed in an extensive fixture list. Notice the large shin pads and the snake-head belts.

THIS MODEL T FORD was used as a delivery van by Roses, the butchers, in the 1920s (decorated here for the carnival procession in 1922). Henry Bridewell, the older man, was probably not the driver. His responsibility in the firm was for the horses that were also used for deliveries.

HMS *DEVIZES* WAS A CARNIVAL FLOAT ENTRY for W.E. Chivers and Sons in the carnival of 1925, the year that Fred Chivers was the town mayor.

WORTON CHOIR OUTING IN A BODMAN'S CHARABANC in 1927. The picture was probably taken in The Canal, Salisbury where most charabanc trips heading south to the coast seem to have stopped for fuel, a break and a photograph.

ALL SET FOR THE CARNIVAL! An Urchfont family ready for the parade in Urchfont in about 1925.

AN ANNUAL DEVIZES SHOW was held on fields in London Road. Here at the show in 1907 Mr W. Holman is seen about to enter the ring for his round.

MEMBERS OF URCHFONT BAND just before playing a concert in August 1907.

Village Shops and Inns

ROWDE POST OFFICE in about 1905. The village post offices were often also the general stores, supplying the food and hardware needs of the community between visits to the town. Without the telephone most people wrote frequent letters and postcards and the post office was their lifeline. Rowde post office was situated just across the way from the Cross Keys Inn.

STONE'S BAKERY AND GROCERY SHOP in Urchfront in about 1925. The business began in 1858 and remained with the Stone family until 1951. After this date the bakehouse, which is on the right-hand side of the building, became the shop and the old shop became a doctor's surgery. The shop finally closed in the early 1960s. This picture shows the firm's first delivery van which had recently replaced the horse and cart.

THE OLD BELL INN IN BULKINGTON photographed here probably before 1900. Ushers' ales and stouts were available and the landlord was John Axford. A note on the reverse of this card says that the two in the doorway are Dolly and little Milly. This thatched and timber-framed building was replaced by the present brick-built inn sometime after the First World War. A few years ago the name was changed to the Well Inn, apparently to avoid local confusion with The Bell Inn at nearby Seend.

URCHFONT VILLAGE in 1900, the romantic rural idyll.

THE OLD CROSS KEYS INN, Rowde, in about 1900.

THE EDGE OF THE GREEN in Urchfont showing one of the village shops in about 1910.

THE HIGH STREET, WORTON, some time before 1920. The Royal Oak was owned and run at this time by Mr Goss the blacksmith who also had the forge next door, to the left of the pub. Mr Goss was a farrier and wheelwright and was engaged during the First World War, like many village blacksmiths, in producing huge quantities of horseshoes for the army's horses. Mr Early of Worton remembers his first job, at the age of fourteen, was helping with this war effort at Goss' forge. The forge moved up the High Street after the war to the Rose and Crown where Mr Goss was again publican and smith. His forge is now the pub's skittle alley and the Royal Oak, much altered, is a private house.

THE GEORGE AND DRAGON has been an important inn on the Devizes–Salisbury road for a very long time. The original building was timber-framed and probably built between 1450 and 1500 by the Bishop of Salisbury. Parts of the timber framing, including a timber cruck truss in the original hall of the building remain, although the exterior was rebuilt in brick in the eighteenth century. The inn was known as The George for much of its history, at least as far back as 1645. This photograph was taken in the early years of the century.

THE AVON VALE HUNT meet outside The George and Dragon at Potterne in February 1916. This picture appeared in a magazine with a caption that included, 'The Government has expressed a hope that hunting shall be continued' (during the war).

THIS CARTOON BY RAVENHILL APPEARED IN PUNCH in the 1930s and clearly has The George and Dragon at Potterne in the background. Ravenhill lived for a time in Bromham and appears to have used local backgrounds for his cartoons on many occasions.

LIKE MANY OF THE SMALLER VILLAGES old Urchfont had far more shops and small businesses than it does today. This picture taken in about 1924 shows two of them, Bond's general stores and the post office.

THE OLD CROSS KEYS INN, Rowde, undergoing what was probably to be its final rethatching, in about 1930. In 1937 a disastrous fire was to destroy the building.

THE OLD PLOUGH INN IN PLOUGH LANE, Marston in about 1905.

THE LAMB INN AT ROWDE in the 1890s. The inn building has gone but the house attached to it still stands.

MR WESTON, THE POULSHOT BAKER, seen here in the family bakery near to the Raven Inn.

THE LARGE NUMBERS OF WORKING HORSES meant a high demand for saddlery and horseshoes and even small villages had suppliers of both. In Urchfont, Harry Fuller was the saddler, photographed here with his staff in 1904.

The Farming Year

CHARLES DREWITT, farm labourer at Manor Farm, Potterne, in about 1903.

CULTIVATING SOME ROUGH GROUND on Bigg's Farm, Marston, with a four-horse team. One man carries a shotgun perhaps hoping to shoot something for his supper during his day in the fields.

POUND COTTAGE (now Hillview) on The Green, Marston, in about 1905, so called because the adjacent field was the village cattle pound for stray animals. The lady in the foreground is Mrs Few.

ALFRED HALE still using horses to pull the harrow at Hurst Farm, Worton, in 1950.

LAND GIRLS WORKING AT UPHILL FARM in Urchfont during the Second World War.

SID WICKS AND TOM MILES lead home the horses after a day in the fields at Horton in 1928. In his book, *Akenfield*, Ronald Blythe noted how men and horses returned to the farm in a strict order of precedence. The younger and less experienced waited down the lane regardless of work or weather until their elders had gone ahead.

A DEMONSTRATION OF A NEW POTATO LIFTER at Wild's farm to Bromham farmers in about 1930. The man with the pipe is the representative from T.H. White's, the agricultural engineers who organized the demonstration, and the man driving the device is Len Paget.

A PEA-PICKING GANG at work in Bromham in about 1908. Peas were often not picked by the farmer who grew them. Fields of growing peas were sold by auction at The Greyhound Inn and the buyer would then organize a picking gang to harvest them. Pickers were paid by the load picked and peas went to markets mainly in Bath and Bristol by rail from Bromham and Rowde Holt. Edwin Wootten, in the centre of this picture, grew his own peas but also bought other fields to pick.

STEAM-POWERED THRESHING at Bigg's Farm, Marston, in the 1890s. This unusual interruption to the day's work by a photographer has resulted in an amusing variety of responses to his request to take up a pose.

OAKS FARM, BROMHAM, in 1951. The farmer J.G. Davis was one of the founder members of the group that now market their produce under the name of Wiltshire Vegetables.

A TRADITIONAL HARVEST HOME PARTY given for family, friends and employees by Mr and Mrs Isaac Davis at St Edith's Cottage, Bromham, in about 1905.

HAYMAKING AT EAST END FARM, MARSTON, in about 1900. The men at the extreme left and right are the Orams – father and son.

HARVESTING WHEAT AT MANOR FARM near Wedhampton in 1951. Redhorn Hill is in the background.

THE OLD PUMPING STATION on the turnpike road (A361) near Shepherd's Shore on Bishop's Cannings Down in about 1900. The pumping station brought water to Devizes across these lonely downs, at this time occupied only by shepherds and their sheep. The extensive use of the downs today for growing wheat crops has meant an almost total loss of sheep on the downs. Ida Gandy, who wrote about her childhood in Bishop's Canning in the early part of the century describes the old downs and the shepherds. Among her anecdotes she tells how many of the local shepherds wore heavy blue cloaks lined with red, which had been brought back from the Crimean War by their fathers and were still in use fifty years later.

SECTION TEN

Special Events

THE PRINCE OF WALES visited Devizes in 1893 to mark the centenary celebrations of the Royal Wiltshire Yeomanry whose foundation had followed a meeting of volunteers at The Bear Hotel. The town was elaborately decorated not only with bunting and banners but large castellated wooden arches as well. These stood across Northgate Street, London Road by St James' church and across St John's Street.

DECORATIONS IN MARYPORT STREET in 1893 for the visit of the Prince of Wales on the centenary of the Royal Wiltshire Yeomanry.

THE ARCH CONSTRUCTED ACROSS ST JOHN'S STREET for the celebrations on the visit of the Prince of Wales.

ON DISPLAY IN DEVIZES MUSEUM is an unusual drum that was made in Bishop's Cannings in 1820. It was commissioned by the Bishop's Cannings Friendly Society from a firm of intrument makers called Bruton in Devizes. As one of their employees lived in the village he was given the job of making it and was to use an upstairs room at the Crown Inn (not the present one). On completion the splendid drum was found to be too large to pass through the door or windows and so on days when the Friendly Society paraded through the village the unfortunate drummer stood by an open window at the pub playing as loudly as he could! When eventually the old pub was demolished the drum was liberated and used in village celebrations for many years. One of the most recent of these is seen in this photograph on the occasion of the coronation of Elizabeth II in 1953. The drum is barely visible in the centre of the group as they parade past the present Crown Inn.

THE WHOLE VILLAGE OF POULSHOT gathered before the school in 1911 for the celebration dinner commemorating the coronation of George V.

A NATIONAL TOWN CRIERS' CONTEST was held in Devizes in February 1912. The panels of judges sat at tables outside The Bear Hotel and contestants stood on steps outside the Shambles Market House and made their announcements. Here the contestants are seen lined up across the Market Place to be presented to the dignitaries before they begin. The Devizes crier was John Nott and the winner of the contest was Frank Slade from Aylesbury. The prize was £5 and the Championship Bell. This may seem like a modest prize but it is considerably better than the special prize awarded for the 'Best Crier from Wilts, Devon, Somerset or Dorset; £1-1s., to be spent in Devizes.'

THE 'CHAMPION VOICE'. Frank Slade from Aylesbury, winner of the Town Criers' contest.

THE VILLAGE OF COATE lies two miles to the east of Devizes and remains a small village community. Coronations and jubilees have always been seen as an opportunity for village and street parties and group photographs. The whole of Coate village is assembled here in 1937 to celebrate the coronation of George VI.

THE PRIMITIVE METHODIST CHAPEL on The Green, Marston, following a reopening ceremony after some improvements in July 1914. The chapel recently underwent more repairs and the congregation posed for another photograph like this, seventy-five years on.

THE COUNCIL DECIDED TO WALL IN THE CRAMMER to make it safer in 1967. The action was so indignantly opposed that it was dismantled again before the job was completed.

MOST OF THE INHABITANTS OF WORTON are gathered in this photograph by the village hall in 1937 at a village celebration for the coronation.

SECTION ELEVEN

Village People and their Houses

THE LARGE GARDEN IN NETHERSTREET, Bromham, of Emily Powney, seen here with her brother Henry Hughes in 1933.

MRS ORAM OUTSIDE EAST END FARMHOUSE in Plough Lane, Marston, in about 1900. The Oram family later set up New Farm in Marston, where the son and his wife are still farming.

MRS ORAM'S MOTHER outside the same cottage in the 1880s.

CHARLOTTE COLEMAN STANDS BEFORE HER HOUSE, Ivy Cottage, next to the Royal Oak in High Street, Worton, in about 1910.

THE OLD RECTORY IN POULSHOT in the 1870s. The style of the photograph is very much of the period with members of the household and friends arranged picturesquely in groups and even at the windows. Contemporary accounts suggest that the rectory was not a comfortable place to live at the time. In the winter it suffered badly from damp and the lawns were under water for much of the time.

A DAIRY HERD make their way back to the farm at Uphill, Urchfont, about 1930. This pond has now been filled in but the cottage survives.

THIS PHOTOGRAPH OF POTTERNE in around 1900 was one of a pair of stereoscopic prints produced by an American publisher, A.F. Jarvis of Washington, DC.

FREDERICK KEMPSTER, THE WILTSHIRE GIANT. Several villages claim this giant as their own and in fact he lived for a time in Worton, Seend and Avebury. He was reputed to have been 7 ft 9½ in (237 cm) tall and weighed 22 st. When in Worton he lived at the lodge opposite the post office and had to enter the house on his hands and knees. He played darts at the pub while kneeling. For a short time he stayed with the Hockley family at the Red Lion in Avebury and is referred to in the Guiness Book of Records as the Avebury Giant. He travelled widely in Europe as a fairground attraction and teamed up with a German giantess for a time. This photograph was taken in 1910 during one of his trips to Germany when he was twenty-one years old. He was in Germany at the outbreak of the First World War and his return to England was only effected with some difficulty and delay, during which time he was taken ill. On his return he stayed in Seend but never fully recovered his health. Although local tradition has it that he died in Seend it is more likely that he died in 1918 during a visit to Blackburn.

THIS OLD LADY IN HER CRISP WHITE APRON AND A CAP stands outside the old bakery building at Home Farm, Close Lane, Marston, in about 1895.

THE BLACKSMITHS' FORGE AND CARPENTRY WORKSHOPS of Mr A.J. Hillier and Mr Hiscock at Horton in the 1890s. Mr Hillier moved to Bishop's Cannings in about 1900 and set up his forge on the corner opposite the present school. This house, Chestnut House (see p. 87), is still owned by his family and the forge has become the village shop and post office. Mr Hiscock is credited with inventing a special plough for chalk soil.

JOHN MILLER THE DAIRYMAN delivering milk to the cottage opposite the pub in Bishop's Cannings in the 1920s. He kept his small dairy herd in fields in Horton Road. After cooling the milk in a simple dairy building in the field, he sold it around the village from his pony and cart. He began with a donkey but one morning after milking, the animal drank a large pan of the hot milk while the dairyman's back was turned and collapsed and died.

JEAN PEARCE AND HER PARENTS by their duck pond at Mansion Farm, Marston, in 1930.

THE WORTON VILLAGE SCHOOL TEACHER at her cottage in the High Street, West End, Worton, in about 1900.

FOXLEY CORNER between Urchfont and Wedhampton in 1904.

THE OLD PEPPERCOMBE MILL, URCHFONT, in 1897, with Mr Stone the miller and his wife.

MRS ALEXANDER, oldest resident of Urchfont, receives a royal greetings telegram on her 100th birthday in 1935 watched by her family and the postman who brought it on his bicycle.

LONG DRY SUMMERS have often reduced the size of Urchfont's village pond but rarely so dramatically as here in 1908.

A PICTURESQUE VIEW OF MANOR FARM in Conscience Lane, Rowde, which was commissioned by the owners as a Christmas card for 1907. The farm is no longer there.

RURAL PEACE AT NORNEY CORNER, Marston, in the early years of the century.

PROBABLY THE EARLIEST PHOTOGRAPH OF BROMHAM, taken in the 1860s, a view of old cottages in Church Street which have now been demolished.

MRS 'JIMMY' HUGHES in the garden of her cottage in The Chantry, Bromham, in about 1905.

URCHFONT about 1900 looking from the schoolhouse down the footpath that leads to The Bottom.

HERBERT FERRIS, cowman in Urchfont in about 1932.

CHARLIE PICKETT took milk from the dairy at Lawn Farm, Bulkington, to Staverton Dairy daily. He is seen here in about 1920.

IT IS PERHAPS NOW LESS WELL REMEMBERED that a force of Land Girls existed during the First World War. Mrs Gascoine seen here in her uniform worked on farms in Bromham.

THE VIEW FROM THE TOWER OF ST MATTHEW'S CHURCH, Rowde, looking over the roof of the vicarage to the High Street.

THE GRANDMOTHER OF MRS DUNFORD, THE COACH DRIVER, outside her cottage in High Street, Worton, before 1900.

WORTON HIGH STREET AND POST OFFICE in about 1930.

URCHFONT BOTTOM showing the sawmill's yard in 1908.

A CORNER OF THE GREEN IN URCHFONT in about 1920. The man leading the horses is Tom Gillett the village roadman. His job was to cut the grass on the green and the verges and to keep them tidy.

PEPPERCOMBE LANE, URCHFONT, about 1900. The lane led down to a stream and Peppercombe Mill. The cottage on the left still stands, now at the entrance to Peppercombe Close.

THE ELLIS FAMILY outside their home, End Cottage, Worton, in 1930.

THE VILLAGE GREEN IN POULSHOT in the early years of the century. A cobbled path ran alongside the road as an alternative course for pedestrians when the road became too messy. The cobbles are no longer visible, being completely obscured by today's much denser growth of grass.

THIS IS AN IMPOSSIBLE VIEW OF ROWDE! The photographer has sought to enhance the view by sticking a field of cows below a real view of the village as seen from the Bromham Road. Such techniques were very common. Postcard collectors are quite used to seeing the same groups of swans or people turning up on different backgrounds in Victorian and Edwardian postcards.

THE ALMSHOUSES IN BROMHAM, now demolished, seen here in about 1907.

WORTON HIGH STREET in about 1900. The cottages on the right form Prospect Terrace and the house to the left of centre is Yew Tree House.

THE HIGH STREET, BULKINGTON, looking east towards Devizes in about 1910.

THIS PICTURE POSTCARD OF WHISTLEY LANE, POTTERNE, taken in the early years of the century was labelled, 'Rustic View'. The view today still looks fairly rustic and the same tap runs.

A VIEW OF BISHOP'S CANNINGS taken from the church tower looking north-east in about 1905. A new village school was built in 1909 in the field in the centre of this view and on its opening day the children walked down the lane to it from their old school at the village crossroads. The old building became the Working Men's Club and is now the village hall.

MANSION FARM AT THE CORNER OF CLOSE LANE, Marston, in 1928. The pond and its elegant bridge are now gone.

THE MAIN STREET, BULKINGTON, looking west from the old cross in about 1915. The pond has long ago been filled in and the corrugated-iron village hall was removed more than twenty years ago. At the roadside are piles of stones for road mending. Many people in the villages remember stone piles like these and the stonebreakers who broke them down to size. Often one person in the village would be employed to do this job using three hammers of decreasing size. Large rocks were dumped at the roadside in heaps and then gradually reduced to the size of coarse gravel by the efforts of the stonebreaker and his hammers alone. Later the stone was scattered over the road and compressed with a steamroller. These roads were dusty in summer and muddy in winter.

AN IMPORTANT PART OF THE WAR EFFORT in the Second World War was that contributed by the Land Girls. Many young women went to work on farms for the first time in their lives and joined a highly disciplined work force. The government supplied the uniforms and a military style approach to farm work. The intention was not only to compensate for the loss of male farm workers but to increase production of home-grown food above pre-war levels. The scheme was highly successful and there are many that remember with some fondness their experiences on the farm. This group photograph shows the Davis sisters from Rowde who worked together on a farm in London Road, Devizes. Nellie, in the middle, remembers well that an added attraction of joining the Land Army at the time was the warm coat and other clothing that came with the job, as clothes for civilians were severely rationed.

POULSHOT GREEN, one of the village's best assets, has changed little since this photograph was taken early in the century. The ducks and geese at this time were spoilt for choice when wanting a swim, there were four ponds in different parts of the green and locals referred to it as 'Poulshot Docks'.

A GROUP OF GUESTS on their way to a wedding in Horton in about 1895. The three in the centre of the group are George, Nellie and Annie Drew.

THIS OLD TIMBER-FRAMED AND THATCHED FARMHOUSE at Close Farm, Marston, burned down in 1956 and was subsequently demolished. The fire started in the adjacent pigsty when the pigs knocked over a paraffin heating lamp.

URCHFONT VILLAGE HALL was built in 1929 and here we see the first bricks being laid on 23 March. It was built by voluntary village labour with materials bought with subscriptions from the village. It was completed in September and there was a formal opening ceremony in November with speeches and a concert.

ACKNOWLEDGEMENTS

Compiling a collection of photographs like this one depends very much on the generosity and interest of lots of people. I would like to thank in particular all those who have loaned their photographs and allowed me to reproduce them here:

Miss F. Bailey • Miss M. Barnes • Bishop's Cannings School • Mr J. Bodman
Mrs Butt • Mr and Mrs Carter • Mr T. Cartwright • Dr J. Chandler
Miss G. Chivers • Mr Ted Chivers • Mrs J. Clack • Mr Cook • CPRE
Mrs H. Davis • Mr J.G. Davis • Devizes Museum (WANHS) • Mr E. Dight
Mrs Dixon • Mrs Dunford • Mr E. Giles • Mr L. Hailstone • F. Haines
Mrs P. Hancock • Mr R. Harris • Mr and Mrs J. Hurley • Imperial War Museum
the Jennings Family • Mrs Knight • Mr K. Mahoney • Mr and Mrs T. Maslen
Ms S. Mearus • Mrs R. Moulton • Mr M. Oliver • Mr and Mrs Oram
Mr J. Picket • Mr R. Pope • Mr Dennis Powney • Mr and Mrs A. Rugg
Mrs N. Sims • Mr B. Smith • Mr R. Smith • Mr W. Stanley • Mrs A. Stokes
the Stratton Family • Mr A.J. Trimnell • the Trust for Poulshot
Mr Tony Whatley • Mrs M. Williams • Wiltshire Fire Brigade HQ (Potterne)
Wiltshire Library and Museum Service • Wiltshire Newspapers Ltd.

Special thanks to Richard Larden for his help in making excellent photographic copies of some of the original material and also to Colin Kearley for copies he made from negatives owned by Wiltshire Newspapers Ltd. Thanks too for the help given by staff of The Local Studies Library at County Hall Trowbridge, Devizes Library (especially Marion Fryer), The Wiltshire Archaeological and Natural History Society and The Kennet and Avon Canal Trust. My thanks also to Mr Freddie Henry for identifying the motor vehicles in the photographs, Ms Nicholls for typing the manuscripts. Finally, my gratitude to all the many people who willingly helped with identification, looked up dates, shared their memories and generously gave time and advice.